So the Light Stays

poems by

Danielle Blinka

Finishing Line Press
Georgetown, Kentucky

So the Light Stays

ACKNOWLEDGMENTS

I'd like to thank my partner Aaron for his love and support. I'm so grateful
to have you in my life. Thank you for reading these poems and pointing out
the best parts. I'd also like to thank everyone who's read and critiqued these
poems at a Write Club meeting, especially Steve. Finally, I'd like to thank one
of my poetry mentors, R.S. Gwynn.

Publisher: Leah Huete de Maines
Editor: Christen Kincaid
Cover Art and Design: Danielle Blinka
Author Photo: Danielle Blinka
Cover Design: Elizabeth Maines McCleavy

Order online: www.finishinglinepress.com
also available on amazon.com

Author inquiries and mail orders:
Finishing Line Press
PO Box 1626
Georgetown, Kentucky 40324
USA

Contents

People Like Us

People like us
are born with a light
so bright
we hide behind a mask.

People like us
get brighter in darkness—
are closer to truth
behind closed doors,
under neon lights,
in stolen glances.

People like us
can be anyone
in the dark,
so we become ourselves.
When we're dancing,
life belongs to us—
unburdened
by expectations, side glances,
and warnings.

People like us
drown our thoughts
with spinning records.
We dance
so the light stays.

Leaks

Your eyes look the same
as they did on Easter morning
when I first sang choir songs
in the dress you said
reminded you
of days when you were young.
My name crosses your lips,
and I know you remember
just that moment
my place in your heart.

Leaks come slowly,
dripping memories from a thin crack
at the base of your full cup,
turning our days into gifts
and disappointments.

Tenderly, we refill the cup,
but the crack remains—
threatening to empty
every morsel,
rendering the cup
useless,
a relic of bygone days.

Your Last Words

Your last words to me
were an unanswered prayer.
I said goodbye
To a screen—
Saw your vacant form
Rise and fall in time
With a respirator.
Your absence left a wound,
Taking part of me
With you.
I never knew I could
Feel so empty, so lost
Until you left this earth
And I stayed.
Is this what happens now?
I just go on without you here?
Forget your voice,
Wait for your scent to fade
From your clothes?
I watch grass grow over the dirt
They used to bury you,
The earth swallowing you
And healing her wound.
But I will bleed forever.

Sunset Warehouses

The tracks run beside each other, twisted metal
Cutting through the soil like a zipper,
Teeth dented, the slider caught on jagged edges.
She paused before crossing, afraid of beating
Engine pumps or a locomotive whistle—
Though the tracks haven't held train cars in decades.
Stepping onto wooden railway planks, she rebelled.
Peering over the horizon, she imagined
The phantom specter of a train engine.

Condemned warehouses lined the streets,
Opposing the skyscrapers and polished bricks
Calling her back to the anonymous city.
Even here, in a forgotten street overgrown by the past,
The city buzzed. She felt the press of people—
A cacophony of voices—the loneliness of being
One in many.

The sun floated low on the horizon,
Threatening to sink behind the Earth
Painting the streets grey and gold—a mix of promises
Hanging in the air out of grasp.

Under the setting sun, the warehouses stood
Along the street like rotting teeth,
Their old brick and stone façades discolored and broken.
Stretched in a long smile, the landscape laughed at her.
It once belonged to the city and its story before
The metal tracks bent, the walls crumbled, the pavement
Cracked to pieces,
And the city called the floors and beams unsafe.
Now, the remnants waited in the quiet,
Shrouded in darkness as the bright city lights
Blazed in the distance.

At sunset, she found herself alone, staring at the old stone bricks.
Bodies passed behind her, but the cold silence of disused walls
Called her away from them, drawing her closer.
Forsaking the glimmer of the lighted city,
She followed.

This

From here
It's easier to see missed opportunities,
Shriveled kernels of dreams left to rot
On your vines.
Days pile up too quickly, the sun
Burning away the drops
Of water in your cup.
You know that life is short—
Everyone is so quick to say—
But you thought there'd be more
Than this.

This.
Routines eating your precious seconds,
Sickness stealing whole weeks,
Entire months.
You crave more
The whole time knowing
This is just life. You exist
And the Earth turns, you season
Your food so it makes you feel something.
You express yourself, leave a mark
On someone, some place, something—
Anything.
You make things
Because you know the nothing.
Anything is better
Than this.

Happily, Never

I grew up in a world
of happily never after,
where the shoe never fits,
a frog stole my kiss,
and the prince
ignored me
waving on the shore
alone
without a voice.

I searched
for my fairy Godmother,
a savior
for my poor
unfortunate soul—
but found
empty words, broken
promises.

With my own hands,
I built a castle,
each carved stone
a crown.

The Mayans

Ruins of civilizations built by human hands,
Claimed by jungle—only to be
Excavated and climbed by us.
Stones crumble, but temples
Still rise from the tree line,
Carved faces call to forgotten
Gods, worship a memory.
Tracing their footsteps, I picture
Them in the moonlight,
Trails of white bright under
A full moon.
I kneel in their temples and learn
Their mythos like truth.
It just goes to show—
What is buried doesn't stay
In the ground.
What is ruined can find new purpose.
Your handiworks are a legacy.
Remember that.

Heirloom

A cup is just a cup
Except this cup is yours.
Painted with dingy strawberries,
Faded green leaves
Chipped
From the day I first reached its
Perch on the countertop.
A day when I still thought
I wanted to grow up
To be you.

Your cup
Holds a breathful of coffee
Bringing me back
Back for more
My morning on repeat.

One day, I spotted its twin
Pristine on the shelves
Of an antique store,
A flaking green sticker
Asking for two dollars.

With the chip,
Is your cup
No longer worth
A bit of pocket change?

When I took your cup home,
I felt its weight
Hang around my neck,
Imagined transferring it
To each new cupboard
Until my days run out.

The month after the smell of lilies
Faded from my black dress
Your cup fell.
I watched it drop,
My heart still,
As it descended
Toward the floor.

It's ugly—
Your cup,
Useless with its sips of coffee,
But I'm grateful
For the cushioned rug.

Windows

The eyes have it.
A scar—a half-forgotten whisper,
Healed more times than a leaky
Memory will hold.
The thought floats
Along a sea of pixels—
A deep blue hue
Among a wash of golden brown.

It peers out at the world,
A mark on your soul,
Reminding of past wounds.
Staring from mirrors,
Photos,
Panes of glass.

It's there when you're
Alone,
Waiting for you to notice,
Haunting each tomorrow
Until one day you
Stop.

Cuts

Carried down faded, empty streets,
Waves pushing against the dam—
Ready to bust carefully constructed walls
Around dirt, grains of sand,
Self-inflicted wounds.

Shell cracked open,
Memories spill, as cut flesh
Reveals pristine, opalescent pieces,
Removed for examination.

Coarse laughter and tilted views
Splinter songs
About whiskey and heartbreak,
As soiled fingers tap along
Against torn jeans.

We sit at one table
In four different rooms.
Each choreographed movement
Lost in translation—
Every moment another cut.

This is the Wasteland

This is the wasteland.
Not so much a whimper,
But a buzz
Humming behind a tattered
Threadbare curtain
Consumed by moths.

Home is work
Left undone—
Wires weaving a trap—
Daily life a means of execution.

Electricity
Dances along the cage,
Illuminating
For a small moment
The horror.

Laying bare the hazard
Of the postmodern world—
The tragedy of the machine
Turning home into fear,
Leveling worlds
Built with human hands.

Flesh torn
Away from bones
Twisted, rendered
Useless in their current state.
Stripped of meaning,
They are pieced together
Into a heartless façade.

The wasteland is truth
Hidden behind a dusty filter.
It crawls from the consciousness

And begs to be heard.
Can you hear it humming?

First Bloom

At first bloom,
Searing rays scorched
My pretty petals,
Withering my dainty blossom,
Bending my weak stem
Back toward the ground.

Wilted
I yearned for future days,
A kinder sun,
Nourishing waters to restore
My parched, seeking roots—
Sinking deeper into the earth,
Searching for strength.

Each crooked root
Became a purpose—
Every grain of dirt
A reason to just be.

I stand tall
On my proud stem,
My knit petals spread
Under harsh sun—
Strong
Against the blazing beams.

Match Head

One scratch against a sharp surface
Ignites a flame—
A fire that consumes your past,
Releasing a spark
Hidden
Beneath thin layers of superficiality.

A flicker,
Your bundled potential
Masked by false intents,
Dormant
Waiting for one swift action,
A single, solid stroke.

Your soul
Springs alive with new meaning.
And a new name.

The Rose is Never Sweeter

I pull on a new name,
Expecting to smell sweeter,
But my expectations
Dissipate
Like dollar store perfume.

Wallowing in stale memories,
I pluck my own petals,
Not wanting love—
Just a second bloom.

Bare to the world
I become
A question puddled in
Gaping mouths—
A life ajar,
Filled with funhouse mirrors,
Revealing more truth
Than jest.

Not a rose,
I am a lapel pin on cheap fabric,
A false face
Waiting to become a punchline.

Artifact

Found
Beneath stacks of dusty,
Forgotten items.

Bound—
Compact, waiting to expand
And disclose a world
Drawn
Across static waves—
A story told over broken
Lines,
Disordered sounds,
Leaking across time.

Voices
Interrupt aching beats,
Press their memories
Into a narrative
Rooted in quicksand—
Falling into oblivion,
Never existing
In a world
I know.

America, Promise

Cast your eyes down toward the water.
Your reflection
Carries you home, deep into your history,
Stretched by tethers
Connecting you to the heartbeat
Of your ancestors.

Above you, puppet strings wait to attach,
Tearing your flesh,
Offering a promise always out of reach.
Your eyes gaze up toward the prize –
Tantalized, tugging at empty white flags
That steal your voice,
Bleed color from your memories.

America
See yourself reflected in the pools,
In jagged shards of glass,
Emerging but dissolving,
Truth turned into fiction.
Alone,
But wrapped inside a cloth woven
By unforgiving hands.

Run faster, you will go further
Caught in circles
Round, round, round,
Urged on by muddled voices
Cheering you to go, go
The finish line rolls farther forward.
There are no prizes here on the outside
Only in the pool, the deep well
Pulling you down into memory
Into yourself.

Planted

Wayward seed dropped
Into unforgiving soil,
Refusing to nourish
Your sprouting roots.

Twisting through stone,
You take hold,
Weaving into crevices
Eroded by persistent waves.

Your crooked trunk
Sprouts bare limbs,
Sparse
Verdant blossoms, lacking
A dress like your siblings.

You face their world, denied—
Apart—
Blooming where your seed planted.

Alone you stand
Bare
To the world,
Lovely, with your
Roots of stone.

Graveyard Flowers

On our third date,
You handed me flowers
Meant for a graveyard.
I followed you past the headstones
While you cried,
Saying you wanted to be
A better man.

The night before, you told me
You wanted to fall for me
But my body was wrong.
Too big, too different
From the girls in your pictures.
You said I was the problem,
Said you hoped you'd be
Strong enough—
Decided you weren't.

You told me to keep the flowers,
Sent me home unfurled and frayed.
I can't believe I cried
Over you.
Can't believe I put those flowers
In a vase and watched them
Slowly wilt
Instead of throwing them
Back on your doorstep.

Self Love

Trailing along
Concrete pathways
Under sun,
Faint stars,
Fickle moon,
I found myself
For a moment.

My longing fled,
A specter of my past.
Being lonely felt like a secret
That crossed someone else's lips.

My own heart
Cradled in my gentle hands
Secure with the only
Love it ever needed.

My beating heart
Stayed its course,
Free of rough hands—
Careless, distracted fingers.
Alone, I kept it safe,
Gave it all the warmth it needed.

Until
Worldly wires
Pulled apart my loose,
Insecure fingers.

My
Heart
Fell.

Stoop Shoes

Forgotten
They sit on the stoop,
Waiting.

Tan leather fades
Under unforgiving sun,
Spiders spin webs
Beneath their soles.

On their last night together
She was happy—
Her heels
Tap-tap-tapping with quick steps.

Until the straps loosened,
Slid away.
She left them
On the stairs
'Til her night ended.

What happened
To make her forget
Her bare feet?

The Path

Alone she carved a path of empty promise.
Each thudding step became a cry of solace
Down roads unpaved, through briars filled with thorns.

Days slipped by, each night becoming darker;
She folds her hands with hope that she'll go farther
But knows it's too late to take life by the horns.

As rain descends and water starts to pool,
All is lost and life's made her its fool.
The winter cold embraces as she mourns.

When darkness settles over her lost path,
A quiet sleep steals away her wrath,
Above the trees her lonely whisper warns.

2020

Days
S - t - r - e - t - c - h
Like blank canvases,
As my paint
Falls away in dry flakes.

I gather the dust
Into colorful piles
That flutter
Away
In the wind.

I stare
At empty spaces;
Watch them disappear,
Wondering.

Was it all my imagination?

Move

My body doesn't move
Like I want.
Limbs stiffen, pain settles its weight
In muscles and joints.
I try to hide the hitch in my shoulder,
Beg my legs and feet not to limp,
Rub the numbness from my hands,
Hope tomorrow is a good day.

This isn't the story I tell myself.
I'm vibrant, vivacious—
I can do this.
A go-getter, I'll live my best life.
Can someone please
Inform my body
That I'm the type of girl
Who does it all?
Just let me
Move.

Being

Just be—
Words come easily,
Action
Catches on time's wheel,
Grinding until it halts.

Under the Moon

Under the moon, she's wild and bold,
Her heart forged in fire and gold
With eyes that beam on darkest sin,
And face masked in a fearsome grin.
She wields an ax no man can hold.

From broken pieces freshly mold,
Her beating heart turned to cold,
She swings her weapon sure to win
Under the moon.

Her fierce justice bravely doled,
She culls the dark ones from the fold
And lifts her voice above the din
To challenge those who catch her ken
And give voice to her tale untold
Under the moon.

What You Wanted

You breathed your last breath,
And every memory I have of you shifted.
Every smile, word, action in your life
Is colored by loss—a short
Life.
So much left to go,
More time for you to bloom,
Time to find your meaning.
I thought I had a lifetime
But forgot
Years aren't doled evenly.
Now, I listen to stories about you,
Look at the pictures
You were too embarrassed to show.
Watch life move on,
People slip into your roles.

I made you a memory
Book to look back on your life—
Can see the light fade from your eyes
As the years tick on.
I look for an ending,
Learning some stories end in the middle.
I go on, knowing.
You never got what you wanted.

You + Me

You're a mind reader.
We lock eyes, and you know
Every word I want to say
But can't. You telegraph a response,
Your words just for me.
We have our secrets
No one else can understand.
Shared thoughts that only
Make sense in the world we created.

Love isn't always like this.
It frays too quickly, pulls
You down into a bottomless
Swamp, drowns you. Eats
You alive while you watch.
Asks you to be someone you're not
And lies, making you think it's okay.

But your arms are home,
And nightfall means a glass of wine
With you.
I cook while you chop vegetables,
Fold towels while you scrub dishes,
Paint watercolors while you read,
Collapse with you each evening,
Content in your eyes.

You followed me up a mountain
Even as our hearts beat too fast,
Followed me on the boardwalk on
Borrowed bicycles.
Let me use your phone to film the sea foam
When my memory filled up with photos of us.
You hunted for spirits
Because I believe in ghosts.

We drank wine and held each other
While a hurricane drowned our city.
With you, I'm safe. Together, we can just
Be ourselves.

Paws

A cat
is a jealous boyfriend,
pressing an insistent nose
against your clothes and skin,
searching
for the stench of cologne
and lies.

Catching a whiff
of strangers
down the street,
"Who were you with?"
Cocked ears
demand to know.

The cat rummages
through your bag
certain
of your betrayal,
always leery
of the Tomcat
lurking around the corner.

A native Texan, **Danielle Blinka** is a poet, writer, podcaster, artist, and performer. Her poetry has appeared in *Pulse Magazine* and has been featured in Houston's Words + Art series. For six years, she wrote for *wikiHow* as an editing fellow and content creator. Additionally, she's written for *Rare Houston*, the Boomtown Film & Music Festival, and several blogs.

In addition to poetry, Danielle writes creative fiction. She's already completed the first book in a young adult series about mermaids and magic.

Danielle holds a Bachelor of Arts in English, a Bachelor of Arts in Political Science, a Master of Arts in English, and a Master of Public Administration from Lamar University.

When she isn't writing, she enjoys performing improv, acting in stage plays, painting watercolors and oil paintings, reading, listening to podcasts, and recording her podcast *Bad Acts: A True Crime Podcast.*

She lives in Houston, TX, with her partner Aaron and their seven cats, Catsby, Poe, Kasha, Willow, Rowan, Fable, and Fiona. You can find her on her website at *www.danielleblinka.com*.

www.ingramcontent.com/pod-product-compliance
Lightning Source LLC
Chambersburg PA
CBHW022053080426
42734CB00009B/1330